A Kids' Guide to
Protecting &
Caring for Animals

How to Take Action!

Cathryn Berger Kaye, M.A.,
in collaboration with *The American Society
for the Prevention of Cruelty to Animals*

free spirit
PUBLISHING®

Library of Congress Cataloging-in-Publication Data
Kaye, Cathryn Berger.
    A kids' guide to protecting & caring for animals : how to take action! / Cathryn Berger Kaye in collaboration with The American Society for the Prevention of Cruelty to Animals (ASPCA).
        p. cm.
    ISBN 978-1-57542-303-6
    1. Animal welfare. 2. Social action. 3. Service learning. 4. Young volunteers in social service. I. Title.
    HV4708.K39 2008
    179'.3–dc22
                                                                                    2008026037

At the time of this book's publication, all facts and figures cited are the most current available. All telephone numbers, addresses, and Web site URLs are accurate and active; all publications, organizations, Web sites, and other resources exist as described in this book; and all have been verified as of July 2008. The author and Free Spirit Publishing make no warranty or guarantee concerning the information and materials given out by organizations or content found at Web sites, and we are not responsible for any changes that occur after this book's publication. If you find an error or believe that a resource listed here is not as described, please contact Free Spirit Publishing. Parents, teachers, and other adults: We strongly encourage you to monitor children's use of the Internet.

Service learning occurs in each of the fifty United States and internationally. Some project descriptions are attributed to specific schools or youth groups and identified by city, state, or region. All efforts have been made to ensure correct attribution. The names of the young people quoted throughout the book have been changed to protect their privacy.

The excerpt on pages 27–28 is from *straydog* by Kathe Koja (Frances Foster Books/Farrar, Straus and Giroux, 2002). Reprinted with the permission of Farrar, Straus and Giroux. Copyright © 2002 by Kathe Koja.

The "Do Something" logo on page 8 is reprinted with the permission of the Do Something Web site (www.dosomething.org).

The "Teens for Planet Earth" logo on page 14 is reprinted with the permission of the Teens for Planet Earth Web site (http:// teens4planetearth.com) developed by the Wildlife Conservation Society at the Bronx Zoo in Bronx, New York.

The "Roots & Shoots" logo on page 21 is reprinted with the permission of Roots & Shoots, a program of the Jane Goodall Institute.

Reading Level Grades 4–5; Interest Level Ages 10 & Up; Fountas & Pinnell Guided Reading Level W

Edited by Meg Bratsch
Interior design by Tasha Kenyon and Jayne Curtis
Cover design by Marieka Heinlen and Tasha Kenyon

10 9 8 7 6 5 4 3 2
Printed in the United States of America
S18860510

Free Spirit Publishing Inc.
217 Fifth Avenue North, Suite 200
Minneapolis, MN 55401-1299
(612) 338-2068
help4kids@freespirit.com
www.freespirit.com

Free Spirit Publishing is a member of the Green Press Initiative, and we're committed to printing our books on recycled paper containing a minimum of 30% post-consumer waste (PCW). For every ton of books printed on 30% PCW recycled paper, we save 5.1 trees, 2,100 gallons of water, 114 gallons of oil, 18 pounds of air pollution, 1,230 kilo-watt hours of energy, and .9 cubic yards of landfill space. At Free Spirit it's our goal to nurture not only young people, but nature too!

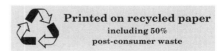

Printed on recycled paper including 50% post-consumer waste

Acknowledgments

As always, the "village" concept comes into play with any service learning publication. To the many service learning colleagues who share stories and examples—thank you! To the youth who demonstrate dedication and passion—your ideas and vision inspire us all. To the ASPCA for their commitment to and guidance in creating humane societies, and to all at Free Spirit Publishing who contribute in myriad ways to the service learning field—hooray! And to my family who provide unconditional support and love—my heart is most grateful.

What's Inside

Stage 1: Preparation

Stage 2: Action

Stage 3: Reflection

Stage 4: Demonstration

What Kids Think
of Protecting & Caring for Animals

"I've loved animals since I was two, and I'm glad to help animals in need of food and shelter. If it was you, wouldn't you want food and shelter?"
—Dakota, age 13

"We left food and water for the animals that seemed abandoned when their families left. In times of war, people can't always take their animals. This is one experience I will never forget."
—Mira, age 14

"During the course of our project I discovered that I was a pretty good photographer. I knew that this would be an interesting project, but I didn't anticipate discovering a new passion." —Malith, age 15

"If we don't help them, I don't know who will."
—Ezra, age 12

"I love the way our service project evolved—from a simple conservation effort, to a community education project, and even to learning about how our local government works." —Bryan, age 16

"It inspires me to help these lonely animals find homes. When I look into a dog's sad eyes at the shelter, I can tell it has been through hard times. I want to make the dogs so well behaved that they'll be adopted." —Adam, age 11

"Training dogs helps them get adopted, but it is not the only way to help out. Picking up litter on the streets can save poor, unsuspecting animals that might have eaten it. Everything you do to help out is important, so do your part." —Emily, age 11

"I can't imagine a world without these animals. When I used to hear about a species being threatened, I felt so helpless. Now I feel part of a huge community of people like me who care and are actively doing something. Everyone could. Imagine if everyone did!" —Leah, age 14

What Do You Know?

How many U.S. households do you think have at least one animal living in them?

☐ 25%   ☐ 35%   ☐ 50%   ☐ 85%

About how many animals do you think are adopted from animal shelters in the United States every year?

☐ Around 300,000   ☐ Roughly a million   ☐ Between 2 million and 3 million

Which continents do you think have animals that are in danger of losing their habitats or becoming extinct? Check all that apply.

☐ North America   ☐ South America   ☐ Asia   ☐ Europe

☐ Africa   ☐ Antarctica   ☐ Australia

For animals, the world is truly shrinking. Places where they can roam free in the wild are becoming harder and harder to find. On the African continent, animals live "in the wild"—though within the borders of national parks, sanctuaries, and game reserves. In our neighborhoods, we often walk animals on leashes or keep them indoors or behind fences. Animals that are on the loose are picked up and taken to shelters. Even migrating animals, such as dolphins, birds, wildebeests, and butterflies, are finding their routes disturbed by fleets of fishing boats, highways, and shopping malls. And many species are being threatened by the climate change our planet is experiencing. What does this all mean? Our animal friends—from elephants and polar bears to puppies and kittens—are growing ever more reliant on people for their safety and well-being. *That's us.* What are you going to do about it?

Starting Now

However you found this book or it found you, these activities will help you discover ways to address the needs of animals in your community and around the world. How? By learning how to **prepare,** turn ideas into **action, reflect** on what you do, and **demonstrate** how you did it. Whatever you choose to do, whether it's participating in a campaign for animal adoption or baking dog biscuits for an animal shelter, the time to start is now. (You'll even find a dog biscuit recipe on page 44!)

"If you think you're too small to have an impact, try going to bed with a mosquito."
—Anita Roddick, activist and founder of The Body Shop

Did you get the right answers?

Here are the answers to the questions on page 2: About 50% of households (that's over 75 million homes) in the United States contain animals. Between 2 million and 3 million animals are adopted every year in the United States. And every continent on Earth has animals that are seriously at risk of losing their habitat or disappearing altogether.

While these questions had "right" answers, many questions and activities in this book are designed to get you thinking, learning, sharing ideas, and discovering new questions to ask. In these cases, few have "right" answers. Rather, they are opportunities to learn, experience, and get involved.

A Note About Using This Book

This guide is written for use by classes or youth groups, so the activity directions assume you are in a group of around 15 to 30 students. However, smaller groups, families, and individuals can easily adapt every activity. If you are using this book on your own, consider finding a friend to participate with you.

Tips for Using This Book

You are holding a written guide, but you will find other guides around you—adults you meet who are involved in service learning, friends and other students working with you, community members who are eager to help—even people across the globe taking on projects just like yours.

★ Keep track of your thoughts and observations in this book. Write in it whenever and wherever you want! (Reflection activities on pages 37–38 are great for ongoing thoughts and feelings that arise.)

★ Stay informed on current news about animals by visiting the many Web sites listed in the book and by paying attention to animal stories in the news.

★ How about starting your own service learning journal in a notebook?

★ Share your ideas, no matter how far-fetched they may seem!

★ Let your creativity inspire you.

Service + Learning = Service Learning

Service:
Service means contributing or helping to benefit others and the common good.

Learning:
Learning means gaining understanding of a subject or skill through study, instruction, or experience.

Service Learning:
The ideas of service and learning combine to create service learning. **Preparation, action, reflection,** and **demonstration** are the four stages of service learning. By understanding how these stages work, you can make plans more effectively to help in your community.

Stage 1: Preparation

Many pets receive improper care because people are not taught how to care for them. Could you help educate others about proper pet care? Of course! What would you do first? **Prepare.** You have experience preparing all the time. When you prepare to make brownies, you choose a recipe and gather the ingredients. When you prepare to teach others about animal care, the "ingredients" are the facts you need to know, and the "recipe" is your plan for action! Make a list of three ways you would prepare to teach people how to care for their companion animals.

> "Any glimpse into the life of an animal quickens our own and makes it so much the larger and better in every way."
> —John Muir, author and environmentalist

Preparation for Teaching Pet Care

1. ....

2. ....

3. ....

....

Now look at the list below. Did you have similar ideas?
- Interview a veterinarian.
- Invite an animal shelter staff member to visit your class or group.
- Search the Internet for information on pet care.
- Make a poster for your school asking kids to submit their pet care tips.

Note: There are many terms for household animals and the people who care for them, such as: *pet, companion animal,* or *animal friend;* and *pet owner, guardian,* or *caregiver.* In this book, we use a mix of these terms. See the section **Do Words Matter?** on page 22 for more information.

Stage 2: Action

Once you are prepared with the background knowledge you need, you can create and carry out your plan for **action.** Most often, you will take action in one or more of the following four ways.

Direct Service:
Your service involves face-to-face interactions with people or animals, or close contact with them.

Indirect Service:
Your action is not seen by the people (or animals) who may benefit from it, but it meets a real need.

Advocacy:
What you do makes others aware of an issue and encourages them to take action to change a situation.

Research:
You gather and report on information that helps a community.

You have already thought of ways to prepare to teach others about pet care. Now, what could you do with the information? What kinds of action might you take? With a partner, list examples for each type of action below. Keep in mind that with service learning, everyone benefits—including the students involved, the animals (who may not say "thanks" in the typical way), and the larger community. Even small actions can have important benefits.

Taking Action to Educate Others About Pet Care

Direct Service:

Indirect Service:

Advocacy:

Research:

Stage 3: Reflection

What is one piece of information you have learned so far that you want to remember?

....

What is one idea you now have that you didn't have before you opened this book?

....

When you answer these questions, you are participating in **reflection:** looking at your experience to determine what it has to do with you. Reflection takes place all along the way: as you prepare, as you do the service, and as you demonstrate what you have learned and accomplished. You will find reflection built into many of the activities in this book. When you see the Time for Reflection symbol, follow the directions to special reflection pages.

··· TIME FOR 🕐 REFLECTION ⋼

Stage 4: Demonstration

Demonstration is the stage where you take the opportunity to let others know what you have learned and what good community work you have done. Are you an artist? Do you like to perform? Do you enjoy writing? Do you like taking photos? Are you a computer whiz? You could use any of these skills or talents to demonstrate your service learning. Circle ways you might want to **demonstrate** what you accomplish:

Make a mural.

Design a comic strip with animal characters.

Create a Web site or blog.

Write an article for your school or community newspaper.

Build a display for a local library.

Put together a video or audio recording.

Perform a skit for another class or youth group.

Create a brochure showing the steps you followed.

Why Animals? Why Now?

Bears on Offense in West, in Search of Grub

Waterbird Population Falls Further

Habitat Loss Forces India's Tigers to High Ground

Open a newspaper today, and an article with a headline such as one of these might catch your eye. Why? Because most people have a connection with animals. Maybe you had a stuffed Teddy bear that you cuddled at night as a child. Perhaps your backyard has woods or prairie where you see animals daily. You might even have a dog, cat, fish, hamster, bird, or other animal living in your home with you.

Circus Elephants Find the Quiet Life at Dubbo

"Kindness and compassion toward all living things is the mark of a civilized society."
—Cesar Chavez, civil rights activist

Southeast Asia's Illegal Pet Trade Threatens Turtles

ANIMAL CRUELTY CHARGES FILED

We live in a world where everything is interconnected. All species of plants and animals (including humans) as well as the land, water, and air around us work together in one cooperative system. When one part of the system fails or is damaged beyond repair, it affects the delicate balance of our world and our existence. Because there is so much change occurring on our planet, animals are in the headlines every day across the globe. And people are rallying to action—finding ways to save and protect all animals, from bees to buffalos.

U.S. ADDS POLAR BEAR TO "THREATENED" LIST

Gorilla's Maternal Instinct Saves Baby Boy Who Fell Into Zoo

"We are the movement and every one of us is important. Without any one of us, the movement is weaker and poorer for the loss. Without all of us, the movement ceases to exist. Who will then care about the animals?"
—Barry Horne, animal rights activist

YOUR TURN

> "As we sit today [discussing this animal], it is important to remember we are talking about the future of a member of our family, not a strange creature that lives in the jungle."
> —Richard Leakey, author and conservationist

The headlines on the previous page are linked to published news articles. Select the headline that most interests you and write your own version of the article. Research the topic by doing an Internet search. Some of the actual articles linked to your headline may be published online; others may not. Regardless, there is related information available on all topics. Then, do the following:

1. Gather the "Five Ws" of your news story: *Who? What? When? Where? Why?* You may wish to include a list of facts, a chart, or a map.

   Who? _____

   What? _____

   When? _____

   Where? _____

   Why? _____

2. Add a relevant quote from an expert or celebrity.

   _____

3. Continue to develop your article while you complete the activities in this book.

4. Find a place to publish your article—in a newspaper, or on a Web site or blog. Or compile all the articles written by your friends or classmates into a book of information and ideas for action to help animals.

At www.dosomething.org, teens are polled about what issues matter most to them and then find ways to get involved. Animal welfare consistently comes up as one of the top three concerns for teens in the United States. Visit the site and under "Causes" click on "Animal Welfare." The site also awards weekly $500 grants to anyone under 25 who submits an idea for a sustainable community action project.

... TIME FOR REFLECTION

Turn to pages 37–38, and choose a reflection activity to complete.

In Need of Shelter

Animals in today's world need care, and humans must provide it. This wasn't always the case. Before large cities and shopping malls took over precious land, before human-made dams altered waterways, and before forests were cut down, animals and humans coexisted relatively peacefully. Animals had plenty of food and land and could survive on their own.

Can you list some ways that humans have made the lives of animals on Earth increasingly difficult? Include at least one challenge faced by animals in your own community.

1: ....

2: ....

3: ....

Without a Home

Your list above might include this reason: Humans have made animals into pets and then sometimes lose them or do not care for them properly. Consider the following situations.

What About Spot?

The Tinker family raised Spot from a puppy into an adult dog that was always fed and housed indoors. When they sold their house and moved into an apartment, they left Spot behind to fend for himself.

YOUR TURN

Be Spot. Write a short letter to the Tinkers describing what is unreasonable about this situation and what will be especially hard for you.

Dear Tinker Family,

_____

_____

_____

_____

_____

_____

_____

From Spot

Kittens in a Tree

Sam and Maria ride their bikes to a park and notice a stray cat by a tree. Under the branches are six newborn kittens. Maria wants a kitten, but her little sister is allergic. Sam already has a cat, two iguanas, and a mouse, and there is a "no more animals" rule at his home.

> **Important!** Never intervene directly if you spot a stray animal. Instead, report the situation to a trusted adult.

YOUR TURN

With a partner, play the roles of Sam and Maria. Write a short dialogue between the two of you, discussing the risk of leaving the kittens where they are, and brainstorming what you might do to help.

Maria: _____

Sam: _____

Maria: _____

Sam: _____

Maria: _____

Sam: _____

These examples demonstrate some of the reasons why animal shelters exist:

- to place adoptable animals in caring homes
- to keep helpless young or sick animals safe and well until they are old enough or healthy enough to be adopted
- to help families find their lost pets

In addition, shelters offer the following important services:

Community Education

When an animal is adopted from a shelter, the shelter provides information on the care of the animal to the family. Animal shelters may also offer literature through the community to raise awareness about how animals are treated and to encourage people to report animals in unsafe conditions.

Spaying and Neutering

Animal overpopulation—particularly of cats and dogs—creates a challenge for a community to care properly for each animal. To help control the population, many animal shelters provide free spaying and neutering services, where an animal's sex organs are removed so it cannot reproduce.

Food and Medical Care

Caring for animals also involves feeding them a consistent diet that is appropriate for their age and health. In addition, regular medical exams and vaccinations are important so animals stay healthy.

As you can see, the overall mission of a shelter is to care for and find a loving home for every adoptable animal that enters. Can you think of reasons why this may not always be easy?

YOUR TURN

Imagine you run an animal shelter. How would you respond to the questions below? Cover the answers on the right while you think of a response. Then compare.

QUESTION	ANSWER
A coworker reports: "Ten new dogs just arrived and we have no more room. We have a few old dogs that are not likely to be adopted. **Should we euthanize (kill) the older dogs to make room for the younger ones?**" _____ _____ _____ _____	Some privately run shelters are "no kill" shelters where adoptable animals will not be euthanized, but others will have to be turned away. However, many city-run shelters are required to accept all animals, making it very difficult to have a "no kill" policy.
A volunteer at the shelter says, "I know many people who would adopt these animals if they saw them, but they are too busy to visit a shelter. **If the people aren't coming to the shelter, how can we bring the shelter to the people?**" _____ _____ _____ _____	How about a shelter-on-the-go? Mobile shelters bring animals and adoption information to the places people gather, such as parks or community events. Also, pet supply stores will often display animals up for adoption from local shelters.

What Can You Do?

Here are some ideas for action. Keep in mind the unique skills and talents you have to offer!

- Locate your local animal shelter and become a volunteer (if you meet the minimum age requirement, which varies by shelter).

- Ask your local shelter for a "wish list" of items it needs and start a collection.

- Decorate your local shelter with art and photos of the animals staying there.

- Use your computer skills to help with a shelter's Web site.

- Write a book about an animal shelter for young children and include photos.

Animals in the Wild . . . and Wild Animals Among Us

Animals around the world thrive in their native wild habitats. The problem is, there is not much "wild" left. To help compensate for this fact, people have created zoos, wildlife rehabilitation centers, nature reserves, animal sanctuaries, and conservation programs. How do these things work separately and together to protect and care for animals?

Zoos

Zoos are places that house animals in contained areas. However, they have changed considerably from the days when wild animals were captured and kept in small cages with little stimulation. Beginning in the 1960s, zoos began to transform into conservation parks. Now, zoos only take animals from the wild when there is a very good reason, like when the animals need help breeding for the survival of their species.

These animals are cared for in natural, stimulating environments as close to their native habitats as possible, and grouped with other members of their species. Zoos today also work to educate communities about preserving wild territory for animals.

> To learn more about zoos, read *A Pelican Swallowed My Head and Other Zoo Stories* by Edward R. Ricciuti (Simon & Schuster, 2001).

Animals at Play

Student groups in the country of Trinidad and Tobago got together with experts from their local zoo to develop enrichment projects involving zoo animals. The group that chose otters created feeding rings and also purchased balls for the otters to play with in the water. As you might guess, the otters seemed much happier afterward!

YOUR TURN

Research shows that animals are healthier when mentally active. Check with your local zoo—are they in need of zoo toys that offer "brain challenges" for animals? Draw your zoo toy design below.

Wildlife Rehabilitation Centers

Wildlife rehabilitation (or refuge) centers exist to rescue and care for injured or orphaned animals, and then release them back into the wild. The people who run these centers are specially trained to know what kind of food and medical care wild animals need.

Learning to Fly

At the Anchorage Bird Learning and Treatment Center in Alaska, people can take a class and get licensed to be foster parents for baby birds misplaced from their nests. One family fostered two redpoll chicks that required feeding every 15 minutes for the first few days. The family had to take the birds along wherever they went—to the mall, to baseball games, to restaurants, and so on. The family raised each chick for about three weeks, until the bird was able to feed itself and fly. Then, the birds were released back into the wild.

To find out more, read *Healers of the Wild: Rehabilitating Injured and Orphaned Wildlife* by Shannon K. Jacobs (Johnson Books, 2003).

What Can You Do?

- Become a volunteer at your local wildlife rehabilitation center.

- Ask the center for a "wish list" of items it needs and organize a collection.

- Gather animal food—ask grocery stores to donate damaged produce, pick up fallen fruit from trees in public areas, and collect unwanted vegetables from community gardens.

- Inform people in your community about the wildlife rehabilitation center and how to get help if they see an injured wild animal.

Nature Reserves & Animal Sanctuaries

Nature reserves and animal sanctuaries are protected lands that contain wild animals inside large enclosed areas. Reserves prohibit development of the land, and keep people out who might harm the animals or their habitats. Researchers study the animals to learn how best to protect them. Where are nature reserves near you?

Trouble on the Reserve

After centuries of coexisting peacefully with humans, some elephants on reserves in Africa, India, and Southeast Asia recently began harming property, other animals, and even humans. With the reduction of their natural habitat and the poaching (illegal hunting) of their elders, these young elephants no longer had proper role models and began acting destructively.

What would you do to help protect these elephants and rebuild their communities?

At Pilanesburg National Park in South Africa, several older male elephants were brought in to live among the young male elephants. With these elders teaching and showing the youth how to behave, the disruptive behavior lessened.

Read *Our Secret, Siri Aang* by Christina Kessler (Puffin, 2007) about a Masai teen in Kenya who is determined to protect a black rhino and her baby from poachers.

You'll notice this seal next to several of the books listed in this workbook. They are winners of the **ASPCA Henry Bergh Children's Book Award,** presented annually to honor books for young people that promote compassion and respect for all living things. Visit www.aspca.org/bookaward for more information.

Conservation Programs

A conservation program, or a "conservancy," protects original habitats so animals and plants can thrive in their natural environment. Consider what fragile areas in your own community deserve protection. Then read what students are working on around the globe.

Following are some examples of kids involved in conservation. Both projects are part of a program called Teens for Planet Earth. (See page 42 for more information.)

- In Shelton, Washington, teens are working with biologists to monitor the amphibian populations and to develop an amphibian protection plan that will serve as a conservancy model for the entire state.

- A group of teens known as "Team Tiger" are collaborating with a zoo in Karnataka, India, to conserve tiger populations by designing and distributing publications about how tigers are hunted and what people can do to help.

Meet Kids in Action: Part 1

Canine Commandos at Work

Fifty middle school students in Merritt Island, Florida, eagerly board buses to local animal shelters every month. Their job: to spend a day as "Canine Commandos," training dogs in obedience. Half the students work on teaching dogs five basic commands: "Watch me," "Sit," "Down," "Stay," and "Come." The rest of the students use clickers to train dogs to stop barking and jumping. Many dogs in shelters are overlooked for adoption because of their excitement, or "untamed behavior," that happens spontaneously when they see people. With training, these animals are more adoptable.

> "Canine Commandos is a great experience and shows me that there will always be dogs out there that need a home. My classmates and I can make a huge difference and change not only the dogs' lives, but owners' lives, too."
> —Isabella, age 12

Taking Giant Steps for Animals

Students in Giant Steps, a program for kids with autism, chose to volunteer at the Shannon Foundation, an animal rescue and retirement farm outside of St. Louis, Missouri. A hundred different animals call this farm home—including dogs, cats, birds, deer, horses, pigs, donkeys, and llamas—and they all have needs. The Giant Steps kids learned about the animals, made lists of needed items, and tracked inventory of farm supplies. They also created flyers, wrote press releases, gave presentations in the community to promote the foundation, and even baked homemade puppy biscuits for the farm's dogs. (See recipe on page 44.)

> Visit www.giantsteps-stlouis.org to view photos of this project, then check out www.theshannonfoundation.org for ways you can get involved.

Meals on Wheels for Pets, Too!

Teen Kimberle Baab noticed that animals living with homebound elders may be missing meals or fed meals meant for the elders. She approached her local Meals on Wheels program in Tulsa, Oklahoma, and, with the support of the Tulsa County 4-H Paw Starz Club, created "Meals 4 Paw Starz." Elders enthusiastically enrolled with an assortment of pets, including dogs, cats, birds, turtles, and fish.

> "This project has definitely humbled me. All of the people we deliver to are homebound and all they have are their pets. Despite their disabilities, they do whatever it takes to care for their pets, even if it means feeding their pets their own delivered meals!"
> —Kimberle Baab, age 16

How Animals Help Us Every Day

Have you considered the amazing ways that animals are part of our lives, helping us daily? Take a minute to make a list of all the ways animals work for us, entertain us, comfort us, or otherwise assist us. As you read this chapter, add to your list.

_____

_____

_____

Animals to the Rescue!

Here are just a few of the ways animals work on our behalf.

Crime Stoppers: As sniffing experts, dogs are put to work with their keen sense of smell. U.S. Customs, the F.B.I., and local police departments depend on dogs to sniff out narcotics and explosives, and find people.

The View from Above: Why do police officers ride horses? Because there are some places a car cannot go, even when there are roads. Also, sitting atop a horse, an officer can be above the crowd at a large gathering, such as a parade, to observe and provide assistance as needed.

Search and Rescue: In all kinds of emergencies—hurricanes, earthquakes, cave-ins, avalanches—dogs are brought in to assist. They have also proven valuable in finding missing or kidnapped children.

Sargent Canine: The military provides dogs with special training to become companion animals to soldiers and help reduce stress.

YOUR TURN

What kind of training do you think is needed for the jobs just listed? These animals can be in high-risk areas. Would they need special clothing, or perhaps locator devices to find them if they get lost? Consider the pros and cons of placing animals in risky situations.

At Your Service

Humans value their independence, and many animals help people with special needs or conditions live full, independent lives. With training that often takes years, dogs learn to assist people as seeing-eye dogs, hearing dogs, signal dogs, or companions for people who use wheelchairs or have limited arm usage. There are even guide *horses!*

> Read *Panda: A Guide Horse for Ann* by Rosanna Hansen (Boyds Mills Press, 2005) about a remarkable relationship between Ann, a teacher, and Panda, her horse companion.

> Create a picture book for kids about a service dog (or another service animal) in your community.

Animal *Therapists?*

As friendly visitors, animals bring joy to many people in nursing homes, hospitals, and class-rooms. Dogs are frequently in this role, but so are rabbits, cats, and even horses. Horseback riding and grooming animals are just two examples of how people with special needs gain therapeutic benefits from animal interaction.

That's Entertainment

Animals appear in television, movies, and stages performing alongside humans. Special trainers prepare animal actors for their roles. Talent agencies exist just for animals, and the animals get paid! However, because horses were mistreated during the filming of many old western movies, animals in entertainment now have rights and are protected.

All for Fun?

Animals used in recreation, as in entertainment, can be a complex issue. For example, horse-back riding develops relationships with humans who, ideally, provide exceptional care. Few horses live in the wild anymore; many horses are bred for riding from the time they are born. Viewing dolphins for pleasure at resorts, however, has caused some concern, since these animals are better able to thrive in the wild.

YOUR TURN

Consider all the different kinds of animals that are part of human recreation at places such as circuses, amusement parks, or resorts. Is this in the best interests of the animals? Research all sides of the issue so you can form an educated opinion. Then use your voice and speak out!

Meet Kids in Action: Part 2

Taking a Stand Against Cruelty

Middle school students in Silver Spring, Maryland, recently addressed the cruel treatment of animals in the food industry. They led a campaign to teach other students how their food purchases directly affects the treatment of animals. Their message: Promote farms, meat processors, and grocers that produce, process, and stock only meats from animals that were treated humanely (with compassion). Students then promoted businesses that support humane animal treatment, raised funds for cruelty prevention organizations, and wrote letters to restaurants and grocers requesting they buy humane. Finally, the students made a presentation to the Maryland Board of Education to request that only humanely produced meats be served in the state's schools.

Your Turn

Find out if the stores, schools, and restaurants in your area buy meat, eggs, and dairy from farms that are part of the Certified Humane Raised & Handled (CHRH) program. Participating farms must meet these qualifications:

- Allow animals to engage in their natural behaviors.

- Raise animals with sufficient space, shelter, and gentle handling to limit stress.

- Provide animals with ample fresh water and a healthy diet free from antibiotics or hormones.

- Ensure caretakers are well trained and knowledgeable in animal welfare practices.

- Require meat processors to comply with high standards of slaughter to ensure humane treatment.

> Visit www.certifiedhumane.org/fact_sheets.html for more information.

A Book of Birds

Teens in Mbeya, Tanzania, have observed the changes in their community. As more people settle in the area, the birds are leaving. Activities like construction, farming, livestock herding, and clearing forests are greatly impacting the environment. Another problem for the birds is noise pollution from people, cars, and music. These teens tell the story of their birds, in words and colorful drawings in a bilingual book (written in both Kiswahili and English) called *A Field Guide to Birds of Mbeya*. "Our research is a way for youth to think more deeply about the natural world that surrounds us every day," write the authors.

> This book is a Roots & Shoots project (see page 21 for more information) and also part of the In Our Global Village project, an invitation to kids across the globe to write a book about their local community. To find out more, and to download a copy of *A Field Guide to Birds of Mbeya*, visit www.inourvillage.org and click on "In Our Global Village Project."

Looking Back:
Historical Moments & Actions

In school you may have learned about the role animals have played in history, or how people through-out history have relied on or cared for animals. Think of two historical events that involve animals.

When in history?	Who was affected?	What happened?

The Purr-fect Pet

Cats were not originally found underfoot in people's kitchens or curled up on their beds. Like all animals, they were once wild and were first drawn to humans through agriculture. As humans harvested and stored grains for food, rodents scavenged for the grain, and cats chased the rats. As early as 1600 B.C.E., Egyptians valued their felines. Cats were considered sacred animals, and were lovingly cared for in life and in death. When a cat died, all the members of an Egyptian household shaved off their eyebrows in mourning!

YOUR TURN

Have cats always been so highly valued by humans? Research to find out:

"Thousands of years ago, cats were worshiped as gods. Cats have never forgotten this."
—Anonymous

- Why were early sailors fond of cats as passengers?

- What led to superstitions about black cats?

- Is there a reason that witches in folklore often had a cat?

If you're working in a large group, divide the research among small groups and have each select a topic. Then, collect your information into an "All About Cats" book and distribute it to people with cats.

Animals Find a Champion in Henry Bergh

Henry Bergh, nicknamed "The Great Meddler," had a passion for animals. He traveled extensively and was outraged by the cruelty done to animals. His belief that "humankind is served by animals,

"Mercy to animals means mercy to humankind."
—Henry Bergh

and in turn they receive no protection" inspired him to take action. Bergh spoke to the New York State Legislature proposing the formation of a society to protect animals. On April 10, 1866, the American Society for the Prevention of Cruelty to Animals (ASPCA) was established. Nearly 150 years later, the ASPCA continues to "meddle" in the grand tradition of Henry Bergh.

On a separate sheet of paper, write a dramatic scene about an animal being abused either today or at the time of Henry Bergh. Perform the scene and then freeze the action, asking your audience, "What would you do?" After receiving suggestions, continue the performance with a "meddler" stepping in on behalf of the animal.

Important! Remember never to intervene directly in an animal abuse situation. Instead, tell a trusted adult or report it to the authorities. Visit this Web site for more information about how to report cruelty: www.aspca.org/cruelty_report.

Jane Goodall's Visions of Africa

As a child, Jane Goodall was inspired by the idea of interacting with animals. "I wanted to come as close to talking to animals as I could," she says. In 1960, at age 26, Jane Goodall was selected by a world famous scientist to begin a project studying chimpanzees at the Gombe National Reserve in Tanzania, Africa. The project continues to this day and, under her guidance, has led to important discoveries about chimpanzees' daily lives, diets, tool making, and childcare. "Chimps [have] helped us to understand we humans are not the only beings on the planet with personalities, minds, and feelings. . . . We are part of the animal kingdom, not separated from it."

"Young people, when informed and empowered, when they realize that what they do truly makes a difference, can indeed change the world."
—Jane Goodall

Read *Up Close: Jane Goodall* by Sudipta Bardhan-Quallen (Viking, 2008) for the full story of how a shy young woman from London went to Africa and changed the world.

When Jane Goodall first arrived in Africa in 1960, there were approximately one million chimpanzees on the continent. Now there are only about 250,000 due to poaching, disease, and habitat destruction.

Today, Dr. Goodall's work extends from protecting animals to addressing climate change, restoring a peaceful planet, and investigating how our eating habits affect the world. She began Roots & Shoots, an international program that sponsors kids' projects in more than 90 countries.

Visit www.rootsandshoots.org for more information.

roots&shoots
a program of the Jane Goodall Institute | www.rootsandshoots.org

Making History Today

Do Words Matter?

If you had a cat (or if you do have one), would you want to be the cat's *owner* or *guardian*? Would it feel different if you called the cat your *companion* versus your *pet*?

> "I am in favor of animal rights as well as human rights. That is the way of a whole human being."
> —Abraham Lincoln

Words matter when it comes to thinking about how we care for animals, and even how laws protect them. If an animal is considered "property," then just replacing the cost of the animal would seem enough if it is killed or injured by someone. But the feelings we have for our pets clearly show they are not just another piece of furniture. This debate has caused people to reflect on what we call our household animals and the people who care for them.

Over 18 cities have responded by legally changing the term *pet* to *companion animal*. In addition, several cities have or are considering changing the term *owner* to *guardian*. Not everyone agrees. Some groups think animals *are* property, and that terms such as these "humanize" animals and could affect the rights of owners.

YOUR TURN

Which words will you use and recommend others use when talking about animals?

I am going to ☐ **buy** ☐ **adopt** an animal.

This is my ☐ **pet** ☐ **companion animal** ☐ **animal friend.**

I consider myself to be an animal ☐ **owner** ☐ **guardian** ☐ **caregiver.**

What do you think about the changed ways some people are talking about animals? Write a convincing paragraph including your ideas and have a group discussion or debate. Can your class or group come to a unanimous agreement? Or an agreement to disagree?

_____

_____

_____

_____

_____

> Get involved in raising this debate in your community. Visit the Guardian Campaign at www.guardiancampaign.org to find out more.

No Horsing Around

Middle school students in New York City learned of the death of a carriage horse on their streets. They researched the issues of working horses in the city and created a petition to educate others about the situation and influence the City Council. They proposed better oversight of the carriage horse industry and limits on where and when the horses could work.

Animals are still being mistreated across the globe. Here are just a few examples:

- Dogfight betting matches put dogs in dangerous and often deadly situations in many parts of the world.

- Elephants are used for labor in illegal logging in Southeast Asia where they are mistreated, malnourished, and often injured. They are also forced to beg for food while in chains, and are abused by owners and passersby.

- In India and Pakistan, dancing bears commonly work on city streets to make money for their owners, who often abuse them.

> Read *The Deliverance of Dancing Bears* by Elizabeth Stanley (Kane/Miller, 2003), a picture book that shows the dilemma of these animals, and lists ways to learn more and get involved.

> Join the Advocacy Brigade! Visit www.aspca.org/lobby for information about writing letters and helping to get bills passed that help animals.

Simply Natural: A Preservation Project

In partnership with Texas Parks and Wildlife, students in Omaha, Texas, learned how to preserve an open field behind their school as an animal habitat. With no hunting allowed on school property, they focused their efforts on creating a safe haven for deer during hunting season. Students provide wild corn for the deer during the winter, and are also planting trees and planning an eco-friendly nature walk and pavilion. The overall purpose? To create a harmonious place for all life to coexist peacefully.

> Read *Don't Shoot! Chase R.'s Top Ten Reasons NOT to Move to the Country* by Michael J. Rosen (Candlewick, 2007). In this novel written in emails, 14-year-old Chase Riley reluctantly moves from the city to the country and confronts the issue of deer hunting.

··· TIME FOR REFLECTION ∃

Turn to pages 37–38, and choose a reflection activity to complete.

Caring for Animals in Disasters

When natural disasters hit, all life is disrupted. Wild animals may lose their habitats and food sources. Companion animals can be killed, injured, or separated from their caregivers. After Hurricane Katrina occurred along the U.S. Gulf Coast, thousands of people had to be evacuated and saving their pets was a tremendous concern. Approximately 10,000 animals were saved thanks to rescue teams. Not all animals that were rescued were reunited with their guardians, however. Some had to find new homes.

The Adventures of Rufus in a Hurricane

EllaKate Wagner, age 14, learned that some pets rescued from the effects of Katrina had been relocated to her state of Michigan. She wrote a picture book to tell the story of one of these relocated pets—a dog named Rufus—as a way to inform others about the situation and encourage help. She then sold the book and donated profits to local shelters. "I learned how something so little impacts so many people. One little donation can help save three or four animals and those animals go on to have a large impact in our everyday lives," says EllaKate.

On Alert in Florida

The residents of Leesburg, Florida, have had their share of hurricanes. Since their school has been designated as an emergency pet shelter, students created emergency preparedness envelopes for the community. The envelopes include a list of items to keep on hand, a list of documents to put in the envelope for safekeeping, *and* information about family pets.

YOUR TURN

What items would you put on a list for families to think about when caring for animals in an emergency?

Check off any of these ideas that inspire you to take action:

- ☐ **Ready to Go!** Help pet owners create "Evac-Packs," backpacks that include a three-day supply of food, water, leashes, medicine, copies of medical records, and pet identification. Visit the Web site listed below for more information.

- ☐ **Inform the Rescue Team.** Encourage community members with pets to visit the ASPCA Web link listed in the box below to order a free "pet alert" window sticker. Notify local rescue teams so they know to be on the lookout for the stickers.

- ☐ **Be Their Voices.** Create public service announcements for local radio or TV stations to inform your community about resources to help protect or rescue animals in an emergency.

> To order a free pet alert sticker and learn more about Evac-Packs and emergency pet preparedness, visit www.aspca.org/pets_emergency.

Learning from Reading:
straydog

Books can help you learn about situations you've never experienced. In *straydog,* author Kathe Koja gives us a look at life inside an animal shelter from two perspectives: a teen volunteer's and a dog's.

If you are working in a large group, form groups of four to read and discuss the excerpt from *straydog* on pages 27–28. Assign each person in the group one of the "connector" roles below. Each connector's job is to lead a group discussion about the story from a specific point of view. He or she asks the questions listed (along with others that come to mind) and encourages group members to respond. Choose two people to read the story aloud (one as Rachel and one as Grrl) to the rest of the group. Feel free to write notes and ideas in the Literature Circle on the following page. If you are working alone, consider the questions under each connector and give your own answers.

Personal Connector:
Ask questions that connect the story to group members' experiences, such as:
1. Does Rachel remind you of anyone you know? How? Have you met any animals like Grrl?
2. Have you been in situations similar to what is described in the book? What happened?
3. How have you or people you know resolved similar situations?

Literary Connector:
Ask questions that connect this story to other stories group members have read, such as:
1. Which characters remind you of characters from other stories? Why?
2. What situations are similar to what happens in other stories?
3. What might Rachel or Grrl say about these other characters or situations?

Service Connector:
Ask questions that connect this story to ideas for service projects, such as:
1. What needs to be fixed in this situation?
2. How did participating in a service activity affect Rachel?
3. What service activities do you think of when you read this story?

School Connector:
Ask questions that connect this story to learning opportunities, such as:
1. What information could Rachel learn about that would be helpful to her in this situation?
2. What questions do you now have about animals, animal shelters, and volunteering?
3. What do you think people your age would learn by reading this story?

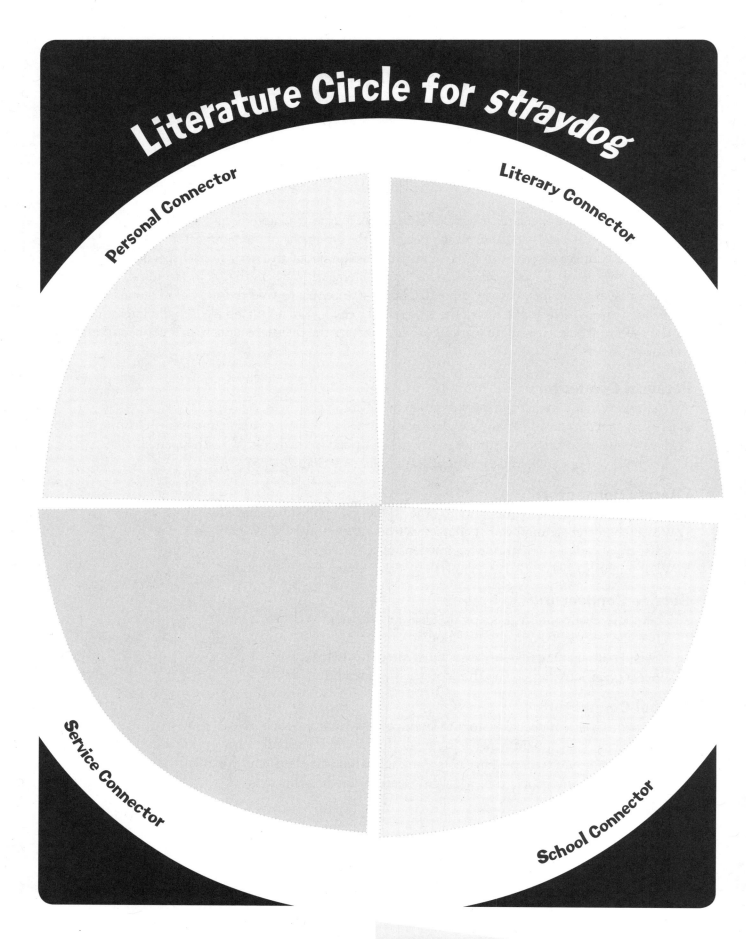

Literature Circle for straydog

Personal Connector

Literary Connector

Service Connector

School Connector

An Excerpt from *straydog*

Rachel, a teenager, volunteers at an animal shelter. When a feral (wild) dog arrives, Rachel feels a bond with it, despite warnings that most untamed animals are euthanized. She names the dog Grrl, writes stories from the dog's point of view, and attempts to find a way to provide the dog with a home. In this excerpt, we hear from two characters: Rachel and Grrl, as written by Rachel.

Rachel's Voice

Have you ever found something and just knew it was for you, the way a key fits in a lock? Nothing at the shelter was strange to me, it was like I'd been born there. It's not a fun place—no place where animals are euthanized (I won't say "put to sleep"; they're not sleeping, they're dead) can ever be "fun"—but it's good work. Cleaning them up, helping the vets. I especially love doing feedings. Dogs are so happy when you feed them. Especially these dogs, who are used to belonging to someone . . . like some family who moved, or had a new baby, or just got tired of having a pet—as if a dog is a toy or an appliance, something you can just throw out when you don't want it anymore. I honestly don't know how people can be so cruel. Melissa (my supervisor) says they have no empathy. I say they're brain-dead. These dogs can't survive on their own: a car gets them, or they get sick, or starve.

But the other dogs, the born strays—they're different. You can't pet them, or even touch them, really. They never got used to trusting people. They're wild. Like the one I see when I get in today. A female collie mix, so beautiful—all gold and white and dirty. She's curled up quiet in her cage, watching everything. But when I get too close she goes completely crazy, biting at the bars, herself, anything in reach, until I back away. Her growl's like ripping metal: jagged, dangerous, and strong. She keeps growling, half falling on an injured hind leg. I see the bandage, fresh and white, against the bars.

Grrl's Voice

cars flashing, splashing by, red-lights, white lights, bright, no one notices me, brown eyes, and wet paws, long fur going every which way: straydog, They say. is that me?

i run and run till my paws are sore, cracked, nails dull against the hard ground, softer on grass, weeds, leaves i sniff and dig through. find a sandwich squashed in a paper sack, meat, bread, yellow smear: two bites and gone.

still hungry. hungry is a place inside, empty as a world. can it be filled? i don't know.

home is no place, a place where i was once, was that home? box full of rags, soft and damp, smell like soap, and little ones like me push, wriggle, and a big one, milk, warm and safe.

then: gone. food, warm, good: all gone. the big one, the box, the little ones and me out in cold and wandering, crying. something biting my leg, biting hard, and me biting it just as hard, AFRAID, and then the thing was gone. i was gone, all gone. into cold and dark, keep moving, moving, moving, alone.

where tonight? a place to sleep, maybe, by the big square metal thing They dump food in. behind it is sometimes safe. sometimes.

some like me live with They, walk with They, tied to They. They have food and give it, all you want—but you have to stay by They, and They can—They do—hit, hurt, drag, throw things, scare…NO. i won't eat from They hands, i won't be tied to They when They can hurt so fast, before you even know what's happening.

so in this wet dark i sit, watching.

Writing *straydog*: An Interview with Author Kathe Koja

"I wrote *straydog* to show how animals can be terribly damaged by how they are treated, or not treated. Even people with good intentions contribute to this problem. They look away from a stray animal, or avoid going to a shelter because it's painful to see what's really going on.

"I resisted helping for a long time, saying, 'It's too sad, too terrible.' Then I started working at events for animals, like adoptions and walkathons, and enjoyed being in a crowd of animal lovers. Now I volunteer weekly at the Detroit Center for Animal Care. I do data entry, so my boss can do other things. I work with many passionate people who give their time to animals, and together, we save lives.

"I hope this book helps you understand that you are part of something much larger than you. You can honor this by caring for something or someone in this world in some way. If you see an abandoned dog chained to a fence, you can respond. This world is filled with creatures who can be afraid like you can, who can love like you can—it's everybody's world. Volunteer at a shelter! Adopt an animal! Like Rachel, find your passion, and go for it."

Turn to pages 37–38, and choose a reflection activity to complete.

A Call to Action

Following is an interview with Ed Sayres, president of the American Society for the Prevention of Cruelty to Animals (ASPCA). His work gives a voice to animals, and provides opportunities for all of us to build caring, humane societies.

> "Homelessness continues to be the biggest problem for animals. Of the 4 million animals euthanized in shelters, half are adoptable. Healthy animals with wonderful personalities remain in danger of being euthanized at the rate of 200 per hour. We don't discard what we value."
> —Ed Sayres, president, ASPCA

"My first word was *dog*. I should have known what I'd be doing many years later! My dad was a trainer for dog shows. I learned early that animals could be part of one's life and work.

"How do we change public opinion about the care and value of animals? We can think of an animal shelter as a community center, rather than a secret place that is dark and scary, by involving the community. We can also recognize the human-animal bond, and how valuable animals are in our lives in ways we can't express. That silent connection between you and your pet is something that only you two can understand.

"Have we made progress? In the 1970s, 15 million dogs and cats were euthanized annually, now reduced to 4 million. Government, veterinarians, and businesses worked together on the 'live release rate'—how many animals go in the shelter and come out alive. San Francisco, for example, once had a 20 percent live release rate; now 80 percent of animals are returned to owners, placed in foster care, or adopted.

> We can think of an animal shelter as a community center, rather than a secret place that is dark and scary, by involving the community.

"We promote: 1) Visiting shelters. Shelters are now designed to be bright and spacious. Volunteers assist with petting cats or walking dogs. A more enriched environment raises chances for adoption; 2) Bringing animals to 'adopting events.' We look for the best human–pet match. Does the person want a 'couch potato' or a frisky dog? 3) Spaying and neutering. Each cat or dog can be responsible for thousands of puppies or kittens—too many to find welcoming homes for. The key is to eliminate homelessness.

"We also want to involve youth as the 'eyes' of animals: Are they well cared for? Do they have injuries? Kids can report mistreatment to a parent or law enforcement officer. They can get involved with animal organizations that promote animal welfare. A family can foster animals for two to six weeks, providing care, for example, for an abandoned kitten. After a home stay, the kitten returns to the shelter for adoption. This can be the difference between life and death.

"More and more people are finding the pleasure that comes with the companionship of animals. Communities that reflect this are my vision for our society."

To learn about the ASPCA's "Mission Orange" program to create humane communities, visit www.aspca.org/missionorange.

Getting Started:
What Does Your Community Need?

The kids you've read about in this workbook based their projects on real community needs related to protecting and caring for animals. Now it's your turn to find out the needs in your community, so you can make a plan for action. Keep in mind that your "community" can be local, regional, national, or international. Your activity can be one that you and others initiate, or you can join in an activity others have already begun.

Use the questions in the following four categories as guides for learning more about animals, beginning with your area. If you're working in a large group, form four smaller groups, with each group focusing on one category and gathering information in a different way.

Media

What media (newspapers, TV stations, Web sites) in your community might have helpful information for you? List ways you can work with different media to learn about animal issues in your community.

Interviews

Think of a person who is knowledgeable about animals in your area—perhaps someone who works at a service agency, a government office, or a school, or someone who has cared for animals such as a veterinarian or wildlife center volunteer. Write questions you would ask this person in an interview.

Surveys

A survey can help you find out what people know about animals and get ideas for helping. Who could you survey—students, family members, neighbors? How many surveys would you want to have completed? Write three survey questions.

Who to survey: How many surveys:

Questions for the survey:

1.

2.

3.

Observation and Experience

What ways are there to gather information through your own observation and experience? Where would you go? What would you do there? How would you keep track of what you find out?

Next Step: Share your ideas. Make a plan for gathering information in the four ways just discussed. If you are working in small groups, each group may want to involve people in other groups. For example, everyone could help conduct the survey and collect the results. Record the information you learn in the next chapter, "Our Community Needs."

Turn to pages 37–38, and choose a reflection activity to complete.

Our Community Needs
What I Learned From . . .

 Media:

 Interviews:

 Surveys:

 Observation and Experience:

As a result of your investigation, what do you think are the most important needs in your community involving animals?

Which method of gathering information did you like best? Why?

Taking Action

This is your tool to begin making plans for action. (If you are in a large group, work together in small groups on this task.) Start by selecting the community need you want to address. Is this need in your school? Neighborhood? The whole country? Around the world? Then, go to Step 1.

 Step 1: Think about the needs in your community involving animals. Make a list.

 Step 2: Identify what you already know. Select one community need from your list:

- What is the cause?

- Who is helping?

 Step 3: Find out more.

- What else do we want to know about this community need and the ways we can help?

- How can we find out what we want to know?

 Step 4: Plan for action.

- To help our community, we will:

- To make this happen, we will take on these responsibilities:

Who	will do what	by when?	Resources needed

Service Learning Proposal

Use the information from the previous "Taking Action" chapter to develop a written proposal of your plan. You can give this proposal to others in your school or organization and to other people or groups that plan to work with you.

Student names: ....

Teacher/Adult leader: ....

School/Organization: ....

Address: ....

Phone: .... Fax: .... Email: ....

Project name: ....

Need—Why this plan is needed:

Purpose—How this plan will help:

Participation—Who will help, and what they will do:

  Students: ....

  Teachers: ....

  Other adults: ....

  Organizations or groups: ....

Outcomes—What we expect to happen as the result of our work:

How we will check outcomes—What evidence we will collect and how we will use it:

Resources—What we need to get the job done, such as supplies:

Signatures:

Project Promotion:
Finding Resources & Telling Your Story

Now that you have an action plan and a proposal, you are ready to promote your project. Write ways you can do so in each category listed below. In the Follow-Up section, decide who will do what needs to be done. If you are working in a large group, form six smaller groups and have each group focus on a category. After you come up with ideas for your category, present your suggestions.

Donations: What is needed for your project (such as flyers, T-shirts, or food)? Who might donate items?

Fund-raising ideas and resources: Be creative and invite community support.

Evidence: Chart your progress for others to see.

Media madness: Press releases, radio spots, cable access TV, Web sites—get the word out!

Presentation opportunities: Consider school and community events, like council meetings.

Partners in the community: Brainstorm all possible partners—even unusual ones.

Follow-Up

Roles and responsibilities: Who will do what?

Turn to pages 37–38, and choose a reflection activity to complete.

Make Your Action Memorable

As you put your plan into action, use this page as a scrapbook to record what happens. Add art and photos or glue in a newspaper article.

What happened today?

 Any new bright ideas to help the project be even better?

One page may not be enough. You may want to keep your own service learning journal in a notebook or start a large scrapbook for the entire group to use.

 Capture the moment! Add a photo or drawing of what you did or saw.

Pause, Look Back, & Reflect

Do you sometimes press the pause button on a remote control? Reflection is like that—a chance to pause and think about your experience from many angles. Sometimes the action in service learning occurs in a day, sometimes it extends over weeks or months. No matter how long your service learning experience lasts, these pages will help you reflect on what you've done. Write the date next to each reflection activity to help you remember the sequence you followed to pause, look back, and reflect.

Date:

What was important about today's activity? How did you contribute?

Date:

Charles Schulz, creator of the _Peanuts_ comic strip, once wrote: "Happiness is a warm puppy." Write a five-word quoteworthy statement of your own that reflects your appreciation for animals. Share it with others—make bumper stickers, posters, or a cartoon!

Date:

What have you discovered about yourself—a new talent, a way you generated a new idea, or something you offered to help others?

Date:

A proverb from the Nez Perce tribe says, "Every animal knows more than you do." What have animals taught you through this experience?

Date:

Imagine a community where all animals are protected and treated well. What images come to mind? Combine words with images to create a visual representation of animals being safe and cared for.

Once You Know It, Show It!

You've put your plan into action and seen the results. Now it's time for demonstration—the stage where you show others what you've learned about animal welfare, how you learned it, and what you've contributed to the community. This demonstration of your service learning can take any form you like: a letter, article, video, pamphlet, artistic display, performance, or PowerPoint presentation.

To help you make the most of your demonstration, answer these questions:

Who is your audience?

What do you most want to tell them about what you've learned?

What do you most want to tell them about how you provided service?

Are there any community partners who you might like to participate in the demonstration?

What form of demonstration would you like to use?

On a separate sheet of paper, write your plan for demonstration.

If you are part of a class or youth group, share your ideas for demonstration with the others you're working with. How can you best use each person's talents and skills as part of your demonstration?

What You've Learned & Accomplished

Take time to think about what you have learned, the service you provided, and the process you used—how you made everything happen. On your own, answer the following questions. Discuss your responses with the people involved in your service learning project.

Learning

What information did you learn in preparing to do service?

What skills did you develop through the activities?

How did this project help you better understand animal welfare?

What did you learn about yourself?

What did you learn about working with others?

What did you learn about your community?

How will you use what you learned in this experience?

Service

What need was met by your service project?

What contribution did you make?

How did your service affect the community?

Process

How did you help with project planning?

What decisions did you make? How did you solve problems?

What differences were there between your project proposal and what actually happened?

What ideas do you have for improving any part of your project?

What do you think is the best part about service learning? Why?

What's Next?

Congratulations! You have completed this service learning workbook on protecting and caring for animals. However, this is only the beginning. You may want to find ways to stay actively involved with helping in your community. This final activity will help you determine what's next.

Write a few sentences about what you would like to see happen in your community.

What ideas in this workbook can you use to help make your community a better place?

On each step, write one thing you can do to stay involved in service.

FYI (For Your Information)

The Internet

Animaland is the kids' Web site of the American Society for the Prevention of Cruelty to Animals (ASPCA). It offers a range of information and resources on everything from pet care to endangered animals to ideas for student action. Go to www.animaland.org.

Kids Planet is a youth Web site and home of the Defenders of Wildlife. Visit www.kidsplanet.org for extensive information about endangered animals all over the world.

The Nature Conservancy is the world's leading conservation organization. Check out www.nature.org to find numerous examples of animals being saved in their natural habitat on every continent.

Teens for Planet Earth exists to help teens protect this amazing planet we call home. Surf this site for reliable facts about the natural world, for the latest conservation news, and to discover how you can make a difference. Interested in jobs on "the wild side" of animal protection? Visit http://teens4planetearth.com and click on "Resource Library," then on "Work on the Wild Side."

The Bookshelf

A Dog's Life: Autobiography of a Stray by Ann M. Martin (Scholastic, 2007). A dog named Squirrel recounts ten years, many spent as a stray. A thoughtful reflection that traces hardships and loneliness for a dog on his own. Fiction, 192 pages.

From Baghdad, With Love: A Marine, the War, and a Dog Named Lava by Jay Kopelman and Melinda Roth (Lyons Press, 2008). U.S. Marine Jay Kopelman tells a story that is both tender and thought-provoking—openly showing the ugly conditions in wartime Iraq, while also describing his growing attachment to a scruffy stray puppy. Fiction, 208 pages.

Hoot by Carl Hiaasen (Yearling, 2006). A move to Florida leads a teenager on a series of unexpected escapades—seeing potty-trained alligators, meeting a renegade eco-avenger, and making friends—all while rescuing small endangered burrowing owls. Fiction, 304 pages.

Vet Volunteers: Fight for Life by Laurie Halse Anderson (Puffin, 2007). Part of a book series about sixth graders helping a veterinary grandmother with emergencies at her animal clinic. This one is about a puppy mill and how the kids help stop it from continuing. Fiction, 144 pages.

The White Giraffe by Lauren St. John (Puffin reprint edition, 2008). An orphaned girl is sent to live with her grandmother at a wildlife sanctuary in South Africa, where she becomes involved in saving a rare giraffe species. Fiction, 192 pages.

A Note to Teachers, Youth Leaders, Parents, & Other Adults:
How to Use This Workbook

Young people have ideas, energy, and enthusiasm that can benefit our communities once they get involved. The question may be, where to start? By giving this book to students or to your own children, you are helping them participate successfully in service learning. The process of completing the activities helps them develop personal skills, knowledge, and abilities required to address the community needs they care about. Kids can use this workbook themselves, or adults can guide them in its use in school, youth groups, or a family setting. The following sections explain in more detail how these groups can get the most out of this workbook.

In a School Setting
This book can easily be used in various ways within a school:

Academic Class: As part of a unit of study about animals, whether local, national, or international, this book provides an interdisciplinary approach to examining this important issue. Students look at civic issues, analyze and compare statistics, read and discuss selections of fiction and nonfiction, develop activity plans, and put their plans into action. The series of lessons can be implemented over three to six weeks of class time when used continuously, depending on the length of the service experience. Another option is to complete one to two activities per week and extend the study over a semester.

Advisory Class: Many schools have a dedicated 30- to 40-minute weekly advisory class meant to improve academic skills, provide opportunities for social-emotional development, and allow for a successful experience in a course of study or exploration. This book allows students to develop communication and research skills, teamwork, and problem solving, while working to make a significant contribution. When implemented in a weekly advisory class, all the activities could be completed in about three months.

After-School Program: These varied activities suit an after-school program. The lessons are easily implemented and include many creative opportunities for expression that vary the teaching and learning methods. Different ages of students also can collaborate successfully. Activities include partner work as well as small and large group experiences. If implemented twice a week in an after-school program, the lessons would most likely extend over three months.

Student Council: If you are looking for a way to transform a typical student council community service project into service learning, this book can be your guide. As students are exploring the issues, they can develop a project that extends into the student body. Part of the project could be an awareness campaign with the leadership students sharing with fellow students what they consider to be the most important information in this book, augmented by what they discover through research.

In Youth Groups
As service learning grows in popularity with youth groups, program staff often looks for activities that encourage academic skills in a nontraditional manner. Use of this workbook is most effective when consistent—for example, one or two times per week—so students know what to expect and what is expected of them. The activities compiled here offer opportunities for lively discussion, firsthand community experiences, creative expression (for example, writing, poetry, drama, and art), and integrated reflection.

As a Family

Family service projects provide opportunities for common exploration and experience. Rather than emphasizing the academic elements, families can use the workbook to guide them through the terrain of the service learning process while gaining collective knowledge and stimulating ideas for projects. It's helpful for family members to approach the topic of helping animals on equal ground, with the youngest members being encouraged to share their thoughts and ideas.

For every participant, this book is designed to open minds, create possibilities, and encourage the lasting benefits that occur when making a contribution of one's personal talents and skills. Each person has value in the service learning process.

Cathryn Berger Kaye, M.A.

Sources for Animal Welfare Facts

Page 13: Information in the section "Trouble on the Reserve" is from "An Elephant Crackup?" by Charles Siebert (*The New York Times Magazine*: October 8, 2006).

Page 18: Information in the section about the CHRH program is from www.associatedcontent.com/article/424086/buy_meat_products_with_the_certified.html, accessed July 2008.

Page 21: Information about and quotations from Jane Goodall are from the following Web pages: www.janegoodall.org and www.webster.edu/~woolflm/janegoodall.html, accessed July 2008.

Page 23: Information on elephants in the section "No Horsing Around" is from the following Web sites: www.elephantnaturepark.org, accessed July 2008, and www.elephantsumbrella.org, accessed July 2008.

Page 24: Statistics and information relating to Hurricane Katrina are from www.katrina-animal-rescue.com, accessed July 2008, and www.aspca.org/site/PageServer?pagename=press_100405, accessed July 2008.

Crunch 'n' Munch Dog Biscuits

Make sure there's an adult to supervise, and read the entire recipe before you begin. Makes 4 to 5 dozen biscuits.

Ingredients:
1 package dry yeast
¼ cup warm water
1 pint vegetable or chicken stock
3½ cups unbleached flour
2 cups whole-wheat flour
1 cup rye flour
2 cups cracked wheat or wheat germ
½ cup dry milk
1 teaspoon salt (optional)
1 egg
1 tablespoon milk

Directions:
1. Preheat oven to 300 degrees.
2. In a small bowl, dissolve yeast in ¼ cup warm water. Add vegetable or chicken stock.
3. In a large bowl, combine all dry ingredients. Add stock mixture and blend thoroughly.
4. Knead mixture on a floured surface for about 3 minutes, working into a stiff dough.
5. Roll out dough to a thickness of ¼ inch. Cut the dough into biscuit-sized bars or use a dog-bone cookie cutter.
6. Beat 1 egg with 1 tablespoon milk. Brush each biscuit with a little of the egg/milk mixture and place on greased cookie sheets. Bake for about 45 minutes, or until edges are golden brown.
7. Leave biscuits out overnight. This makes them hard and crunchy.

Important: Before offering biscuits, be sure to check first with the dog's caregiver to make sure it's okay for the animal to eat them. Some dogs have allergies to wheat or other foods.